# Jesus Calling®

## BIBLE STUDY

# PRACTICING THANKFULNESS

### SIX SESSIONS

# SARAH YOUNG

with Karen Lee-Thorp and Kris Bearss

HarperChristian Resources

*Jesus Calling® Bible Study: Practicing Thankfulness*

Copyright © 2017, 2024 by Sarah Young

Portions of this book were adapted and excerpted from *Giving Thanks* 9780310083658.

Published in Grand Rapids, Michigan, by HarperChristian Resources. HarperChristian Resources is a registered trademark of HarperCollins Christian Publishing, Inc.

Requests for information should be addressed to customercare@harpercollins.com.

ISBN 978-0-310-16687-0 (softcover)

Special thanks to Kris Bearss for her editorial work and content contributions to this study.

HarperChristian Resources titles may be purchased in bulk for church, business, fundraising, or ministry use. For information, please email ResourceSpecialist@ChurchSource.com.

First Printing October 2024 / Printed in the United States of America

24 25 26 27 28  LBC  5 4 3 2 1

# Contents

Introduction      v

Session 1   Open Your Eyes to God's Abundance      1
*Genesis 2:8–9, 15–17; 3:1–8*

Session 2   Guarding Against Grumbling      15
*Exodus 16:1–20, 31*

Session 3   The Gift of God's Presence      31
*Psalm 107:1–32*

Session 4   Thankful in Times of Trial      47
*James 1:2–4; Philippians 4:4–7*

Session 5   Count Your Blessings      61
*Ephesians 1:3–14*

Session 6   Celebrating Your Life in Christ      77
*1 Corinthians 15:14–15, 17–24*

Leader's Notes      91

# Introduction

From Genesis to Revelation, the Bible is rich with expressions of joy and thankfulness. Think of Joseph, giving his two sons names that celebrated the Lord's redemption (Genesis 41:50–52). Hannah, rejoicing over God's answer to her years of prayers for a son (1 Samuel 2:1–10). Nehemiah, leading the people of God in a huge dedication service at the rebuilding of the wall of Jerusalem (Nehemiah 12:27–47). The leper who Jesus healed (Luke 17:11–19). Jesus Himself, who publicly gave thanks to His Father in heaven before feeding the five thousand (John 6:11). The twenty-four elders, worshiping before the throne of God (Revelation 11:16–17). And, of course, the writers of the Psalms, who testified again and again of God's works and character with moving words such as these:

- "I will give thanks to you, Lord, with all my heart; I will tell of all your wonderful deeds" (9:1).
- "Praise be to the Lord, to God our Savior, who daily bears our burdens" (68:19).
- "Let all those who seek You rejoice and be glad in You; and let those who love Your salvation say continually, 'Let God be magnified!'" (70:4 NKJV).

God's Word bears witness of expressions and examples of the opposite too—of ungrateful or resentful attitudes surfacing among His people. And it wasn't just the Israelites in the wilderness either! A close look at the lives of men and women like Moses, Sarah, Rachel, Naomi, Elijah, and some of Jesus' disciples indicates that even they struggled to be thankful at times, just as we all do. Yet as their stories (and ours) unfold, we see the truth: *practicing thankfulness is a means to the renewed mind and life that God makes possible for everyone who puts their faith in Christ.* If we're willing to give the Word of God precedence in our lives—studying it, trusting it, heeding it—the Holy Spirit will faithfully, persistently change us from being worriers and complainers to being *rejoicers.* He will change us into people who practice thankfulness each day out of the overflow of the heart, recognizing God's mercies and kindnesses and living in anticipation of His continuing goodness and care.

With our hearts attuned to thanksgiving, the Holy Spirit moves in us to consider, to respond, and to be changed in powerful ways. It's a work that only God can do. The great news is, it's work that He *loves* to do so that we will draw closer to Him in love and trust, glorifying Him every day of our lives.

## The Goal of This Study

The *Practicing Thankfulness Bible Study* offers you a chance to lay down your cares, enter God's Presence, and hear Him speak through His Word. The study is designed to help you meditate on the words of Scripture and hear them not just as words said to people long ago but as words said to you today in the here and now. We encounter the living God as He speaks through the Scriptures. God has spoken to us through the lives of other believers in both the Old and New Testaments, and particularly through His Son, Jesus Christ. The New Testament gives us the chance to walk with Jesus, see what He does, and hear Him speak into the sometimes-confusing or upsetting situations in which we find ourselves. According to the author of Hebrews,

> In the past God spoke to our ancestors through the prophets at many times and in various
> ways, but in these last days he has spoken to us by his Son, whom he appointed heir of all
> things, and through whom also he made the universe. The Son is the radiance of God's glory
> and the exact representation of his being, sustaining all things by his powerful word. (1:1–3)

With every session, you will get to read excerpts from the *Jesus Calling* devotional that relate to biblical themes. More importantly, you'll spend time silently studying a

passage of Scripture, and then, if you're meeting with others—a friend, perhaps, or a study group—openly sharing your insights and hearing what others discovered. In this way, you will learn how to make more space in your life for the Spirit of God to speak to you through the Word of God and the people of God.

## The Flow of Each Session

Each session of this study guide contains the following elements:

- WELCOME. This brief opener sets the tone for the material you'll be studying, highlighting an introductory thought or idea about practicing thankfulness to help you start thinking about the session theme.

- CONNECT. The two questions in this section connect the thankfulness theme of the session to your own past or present experience. If you've had a busy day and your mind is full of distractions, these questions can help you better focus. And if you're meeting with anyone else, these questions will serve as an icebreaker, allowing you to get to know one another more deeply.

- EXPERIENCE. Here you will find two selected readings from *Jesus Calling* along with some questions for reflection. This is your chance to think through the principles of thankfulness within the *Jesus Calling* devotions and even talk about them with others. Can you relate to what each reading describes? What insights from God's Word does it shed light on? How does it motivate you to put gratitude into practice? This section will assist you in applying these principles to your everyday habits.

- DISCUSS. Next, you'll explore one or more Scripture passages that take you further into the session's focus on thankfulness. If you are studying this material with anyone else, discuss together what the verses mean.

- **RESPOND.** In addition to exploring each Bible passage, you will have the opportunity to thoughtfully respond by spending some time in silence, letting God speak into your life through His Word.

- **PRACTICE.** Finally, you will find five days' worth of suggested Scripture passages that you can pray through and put into action on your own during the week. Suggested questions for additional study and reflection are provided.

## For Leaders

If you are leading a group through this study, please see the Leader's Notes at the end of the guide. You'll find background on the design of the study as well as suggested answers for some of the study questions.

SESSION 1

# Open Your Eyes to God's Abundance

## Welcome

What is your view of thankfulness? Do you see it as, "Some people are just born thankful—and others aren't"? Or maybe, "Thankfulness arises from blessing—the more you're blessed, the more thankful you'll be"? The truth is, thankfulness is a skill you can develop and improve on with practice. It begins with asking the Spirit of God to open the eyes of your heart, and you, in turn, pausing regularly to notice and reflect on God's goodness and faithfulness in your life.

Many people choose to view life through the lens of deprivation, keeping a mental inventory of everything they don't have and worrying that there won't be enough for them. But a life with Jesus means looking through a different lens—a wide-angle one—where you notice everything you *do* have and increasingly learn to trust that God is actively providing for you, just as He has promised.

In this session, you will see the difference it makes to choose to view life through the lens of God's abundance and to start living with His goodness in mind.

## Connect

If you are doing this study with a group and any of the members don't know each other, take a few minutes to first introduce yourselves. Then use the following questions to begin to connect with the session theme—and with each other:

1. *What is one thing for which you're thankful to God?*

**2. How challenging would it be for you to come up with ten things for which you're thankful? Why do you think it's easy or hard for you?**

---

---

---

## Experience

Read each of these devotions from *Jesus Calling* and then answer the questions that follow.

Bring Me the sacrifice of thanksgiving. Take nothing for granted, not even the rising of the sun. Before Satan tempted Eve in the Garden of Eden, thankfulness was as natural as breathing. Satan's temptation involved pointing Eve to the one thing that was forbidden her. The garden was filled with luscious, desirable fruits, but Eve focused on the one fruit she couldn't have rather than being thankful for the many good things freely available. This negative focus darkened her mind, and she succumbed to temptation.

When you focus on what you don't have or on situations that displease you, your mind also becomes darkened. You take for granted life, salvation, sunshine, flowers, and countless other gifts from Me. You look for what is wrong and refuse to enjoy life until that is "fixed." When you approach Me with thanksgiving, the Light of My Presence pours into you, transforming you through and through. *Walk in the Light* with Me by practicing the discipline of thanksgiving.

—FROM JESUS CALLING, APRIL 6

*3. What was Eve's mistake that shifted her away from practicing thankfulness?*

_____

_____

_____

*4. What's wrong with focusing on what you don't have?*

_____

_____

_____

Let Me teach you thankfulness. Begin by acknowledging that everything—all your possessions and all that you are—belongs to Me. The dawning of each new day is a gift from Me, not to be taken for granted. The earth is vibrantly alive with My blessings, giving vivid testimony to My Presence. If you slow down your pace of life, you can find Me anywhere.

Some of My most precious children have been laid aside in sickbeds or shut away in prisons. Others have voluntarily learned the discipline of spending time alone with Me. The secret of being thankful is learning to see everything from My perspective. My world is your classroom. *My Word is a lamp to your feet and a light for your path.*

—FROM JESUS CALLING, *APRIL 29*

*5. What ideas about fostering greater thankfulness in your life do you gain from this reading?*

_____

_____

_____

**6.** *Name one practice you can incorporate into your life that will widen your lens to see things from God's perspective. What would help you acknowledge how He blesses and provides for you?*

_____

_____

_____

## Discuss

Read aloud the following passage from Genesis 2 and 3. The woman in the story is Eve, the man is Adam, and the serpent is Satan.

> 2:8 Now the LORD God had planted a garden in the east, in Eden; and there he put the man he had formed. 9 The LORD God made all kinds of trees grow out of the ground—trees that were pleasing to the eye and good for food. In the middle of the garden were the tree of life and the tree of the knowledge of good and evil. . . .
>
> 15 The LORD God took the man and put him in the Garden of Eden to work it and take care of it. 16 And the LORD God commanded the man, "You are free to eat from any tree in the garden; 17 but you must not eat from the tree of the knowledge of good and evil, for when you eat from it you will certainly die." . . .
>
> 3:1 Now the serpent was more crafty than any of the wild animals the LORD God had made. He said to the woman, "Did God really say, 'You must not eat from any tree in the garden'?"
>
> 2 The woman said to the serpent, "We may eat fruit from the trees in the garden, 3 but God did say, 'You must not eat fruit from the tree that is in the middle of the garden, and you must not touch it, or you will die.'"
>
> 4 "You will not certainly die," the serpent said to the woman. 5 "For God

knows that when you eat from it your eyes will be opened, and you will be like God, knowing good and evil."

⁶ When the woman saw that the fruit of the tree was good for food and pleasing to the eye, and also desirable for gaining wisdom, she took some and ate it. She also gave some to her husband, who was with her, and he ate it. ⁷ Then the eyes of both of them were opened, and they realized they were naked; so they sewed fig leaves together and made coverings for themselves.

⁸ Then the man and his wife heard the sound of the LORD God as he was walking in the garden in the cool of the day, and they hid from the LORD God among the trees of the garden.

**7. What did Satan claim would happen if Eve ate the forbidden fruit? What actually happened when she and Adam ate it? Explain.**

_____

_____

_____

_____

**8. How would thankfulness have changed Eve's thought process when she "saw that the fruit of the tree was good for food and pleasing to the eye" (Genesis 3:6)?**

_____

_____

_____

_____

## Respond

**9.** *What are the things in your life—the things you want but don't have, or that you don't want but do have—that threaten to deprive you of thankfulness?*

_____

_____

_____

**10.** *How would applying an intentional "thankful perspective" affect your current situation?*

_____

_____

_____

**11.** *Reread the passage aloud. Then take two minutes of silence, prayerfully considering how God might want you to further respond to what you have read in His Word. If you're meeting with a group, the leader will keep track of time. Be open to sharing what came to you in the silence.*

_____

_____

_____

**12.** *What was it like for you to sit in silence with the passage? Did soaking it in like this help you understand it better than before?*

_____

_____

_____

**13.** *If you're meeting with a group or with a friend, how can they pray for you? If you're using this study on your own, what would you like to say to God right now?*

---------------------------------------------------------------------------------

---------------------------------------------------------------------------------

---------------------------------------------------------------------------------

## Practice ————————————————————————————————

The theme of each Scripture passage you will read this week focuses on widening the lens of your physical and spiritual eyes to be more thankful for God's abundance in your life. Read each passage slowly, pausing to think about what is being said. Rather than approaching this as an assignment to complete, think of it as an opportunity to meet with the One who loves you most.

# Day 1

*Read Ephesians 5:15–20. In this passage, Paul discussed the need to live wisely in the midst of evil days. What examples of wise living did he list?*

---------------------------------------------------------------------------------

---------------------------------------------------------------------------------

---------------------------------------------------------------------------------

*Why is the practice of giving thanks for everything an example of wise and careful living?*

---------------------------------------------------------------------------------

---------------------------------------------------------------------------------

---------------------------------------------------------------------------------

*How is the choice to look for God's abundance and give Him thanks the opposite of living foolishly?*

---
---
---

*Why are the practices of "always" giving thanks to God the Father and giving thanks "for everything" (verse 20) so important?*

---
---
---

Ask God to help you grow wiser in the way you live by developing a consistent habit of thankfulness.

## Day 2

*Read Luke 9:16 and 22:17–19. Jesus had a habit of giving thanks over a meal before He distributed the food to others. Why do you think He did this?*

---
---
---

*Do you regularly give thanks to God before you eat . . . or only some of the time? If this isn't yet part of your consistent practice, what affects it? Is it a failure to remember? Do you let your environment or who you're with influence you? Is it something else? Explore this.*

_____

_____

_____

*What difference would it make if you gave thanks even over snacks, or when you brought groceries into your kitchen? Does that seem too extreme? Why or why not?*

_____

_____

_____

*What are some other ways you could thank God, "whether in word or deed" (Colossians 3:17), more often as you go through your day?*

_____

_____

_____

Take a moment to gratefully acknowledge God for the food you have eaten today and for the resources He has given to you. Remember in prayer those who are in need in the world.

# Day 3

*Read 2 Corinthians 9:6–11. In this passage, Paul discussed how your own generosity with what you have received from God can spark thankfulness in other people. Do you tend to think you have received abundantly from Him and can afford to be generous with others? Or do you more often think you have barely received enough and can't afford to be generous? Explain your thoughts.*

_____

_____

_____

*What leads you to see your situation in either of these ways?*

_____

_____

_____

*How does a wide lens of abundance or a narrow lens of scarcity affect your choices about sharing your resources (your time, your talents, your treasures)?*

_____

_____

_____

*What are a couple of ways you can practice greater thankfulness in your giving?*

_____

_____

_____

Talk with God about your sense of abundance or scarcity and ask Him to help you see His provision from His perspective.

## Day 4

*Read 1 Timothy 4:1–5. In this passage, Paul warned against the idea (among other things) that Christians should abstain from certain foods because they are religiously impure. What did Paul have to say about such teachings (verse 2)?*

_____

_____

_____

*In refuting this belief, what positive things did Paul say about the abundance God has made available?*

_____

_____

_____

*Why did Paul emphasize thanksgiving twice (verses 3–4)?*

_____

_____

_____

*What do you think Paul meant when he said food is "consecrated by the word of God and prayer" (verse 5)? Why should that make us thankful?*

_____

_____

_____

In recognition of the truth that "everything God created is good, and nothing is to be rejected if it is received with thanksgiving" (verse 4), thank God for the abundance of good things He sent your way today, naming them specifically.

## Day 5

*Read Daniel 6:6–10. During Daniel's time, a law was passed in Persia that no one could worship any god except the king for thirty days. Even though Daniel was a high-ranking official in the king's court, he chose to ignore the law. Why do you think giving thanks to God multiple times a day was so important to him?*

_____

_____

_____

*What are some possible reasons that Daniel opened his windows "toward Jerusalem" when he did this (verse 10)? Why didn't he try to conceal his actions if he knew they were against the law?*

_____

_____

_____

*Would you put off expressing thankfulness to God for thirty days if the law required it? Why or why not?*

_____

_____

_____

*Read the rest of Daniel 6. What impact did Daniel's choice to continue thanking God have on his leader, the king? Imagine how your choice to (a) open your eyes to God's abundance and (b) recognize it with thankfulness might impact those around you.*

_____

_____

_____

_____

Be intentional about setting aside at least three times during this day to thank God.

# Guarding Against Grumbling

The great enemy of thankfulness is discontentment, or feeling sorry for yourself. Sometimes this takes the form of overt anger. Often, it shows up as grumpiness or a negative outlook. At other times, it appears more like sadness or discouragement. In any case, this much is certain: if you carry around a spirit of discontentment long enough, you will begin to "leak" self-pity like a bag of rotting apples in the sweltering sun. And before you know it, you are putting a voice to it—by grumbling and complaining.

Grumbling is not godly sorrow. It's an expression of resentment toward God for what He has allowed to happen in your life. Put simply, it's blaming Him. In this session, you're going to take aim at grumbling (as well as the discontentment that hides behind it) and ask God to help you guard—and then redirect—your heart through the practice of thankfulness.

## Connect

**1. *What does feeling sorry for yourself look like in your life?***

_____

_____

_____

_____

**2. In what situations are you most likely to succumb to grumbling and self-pity?**

_____

_____

_____

## Experience

Be on guard against the pit of self-pity. When you are weary or unwell, this demonic trap is the greatest danger you face. Don't even go near the edge of the pit. Its edges crumble easily, and before you know it, you are on the way down. It is ever so much harder to get out of the pit than to keep a safe distance from it. That is why I tell you to be on guard.

There are several ways to protect yourself from self-pity. When you are occupied with praising and thanking Me, it is impossible to feel sorry for yourself. Also, the closer you live to Me, the more distance there is between you and the pit. Live in the Light of My Presence by _fixing your eyes on Me_. Then you will be able _to run with endurance the race that is set before you_, without stumbling or falling.

—FROM JESUS CALLING, FEBRUARY 23

**3. What makes self-pity such a dangerous trap for believers in Christ?**

_____

_____

_____

**4.** *How does a daily practice of thankfulness to God protect you from self-pity?*

_____

_____

_____

_____

Let thankfulness temper all your thoughts. A thankful mind-set keeps you in touch with Me. I hate it when My children grumble, casually despising My sovereignty. Thankfulness is a safeguard against this deadly sin. Furthermore, a grateful attitude becomes a grid through which you perceive life. Gratitude enables you to see the Light of My Presence shining on all your circumstances. Cultivate a thankful heart, for this glorifies Me and fills you with Joy.

—FROM JESUS CALLING, MARCH 25

**5.** *What are some ways you can build up your defenses against grumbling and allow thankfulness to habitually temper your thoughts? How can such a mind-set keep you in touch with God throughout the day?*

_____

_____

_____

_____

**6.** *A grateful attitude can become not only a protection but also a grid through which you perceive life. Give an example of how this might work in practice.*

---
---
---
---

## Discuss

Read aloud the following passage from Exodus 16. The Israelites had formerly been slaves in Egypt, doing hard labor and making bricks to build a city. When the people cried out to God, He sent plagues against Egypt until Pharaoh allowed them to leave. The Lord then appointed Moses, along with his brother, Aaron, to lead the people out of Egypt. As the story picks up in this passage, the Israelites are crossing a desert region on the way to the fertile land that God promised to give them.

[1] The whole Israelite community set out from Elim and came to the Desert of Sin, which is between Elim and Sinai, on the fifteenth day of the second month after they had come out of Egypt. [2] In the desert the whole community grumbled against Moses and Aaron. [3] The Israelites said to them, "If only we had died by the Lord's hand in Egypt! There we sat around pots of meat and ate all the food we wanted, but you have brought us out into this desert to starve this entire assembly to death."

[4] Then the Lord said to Moses, "I will rain down bread from heaven for you. The people are to go out each day and gather enough for that day. In this way I will test them and see whether they will follow my instructions. [5] On the sixth day they are to prepare what they bring in, and that is to be twice as much as they gather on the other days."

⁶ So Moses and Aaron said to all the Israelites, "In the evening you will know that it was the LORD who brought you out of Egypt, ⁷ and in the morning you will see the glory of the LORD, because he has heard your grumbling against him. Who are we, that you should grumble against us?" ⁸ Moses also said, "You will know that it was the LORD when he gives you meat to eat in the evening and all the bread you want in the morning, because he has heard your grumbling against him. Who are we? You are not grumbling against us, but against the LORD."

⁹ Then Moses told Aaron, "Say to the entire Israelite community, 'Come before the LORD, for he has heard your grumbling.'"

¹⁰ While Aaron was speaking to the whole Israelite community, they looked toward the desert, and there was the glory of the LORD appearing in the cloud.

¹¹ The LORD said to Moses, ¹² "I have heard the grumbling of the Israelites. Tell them, 'At twilight you will eat meat, and in the morning you will be filled with bread. Then you will know that I am the LORD your God.'"

¹³ That evening quail came and covered the camp, and in the morning there was a layer of dew around the camp. ¹⁴ When the dew was gone, thin flakes like frost on the ground appeared on the desert floor. ¹⁵ When the Israelites saw it, they said to each other, "What is it?" For they did not know what it was.

Moses said to them, "It is the bread the LORD has given you to eat. ¹⁶ This is what the LORD has commanded: 'Everyone is to gather as much as they need. Take an omer for each person you have in your tent.'"

¹⁷ The Israelites did as they were told; some gathered much, some little. ¹⁸ And when they measured it by the omer, the one who gathered much did not have too much, and the one who gathered little did not have too little. Everyone had gathered just as much as they needed.

¹⁹ Then Moses said to them, "No one is to keep any of it until morning."

²⁰ However, some of them paid no attention to Moses; they kept part of it until morning, but it was full of maggots and began to smell. So Moses was angry with them. . . .

³¹ The people of Israel called the bread manna. It was white like coriander seed and tasted like wafers made with honey.

*7. Under the Egyptians, the Israelites had been slaves who were beaten if they didn't meet their daily quota of bricks (Exodus 5:6–18). Once they were freed, however, they remembered Egypt in a different light. What did they now say about their time there (Exodus 16:3)? What attitude toward the past and the present do their words reflect?*

_____

_____

_____

*8. Have you ever complained about the present in comparison with the past? If so, what did you complain about? If you're not typically a complainer, what are you sometimes tempted to complain about?*

_____

_____

_____

## Respond

*9. How did the Lord provide for His people in the desert? (Don't forget to consider the answers beyond the surface.)*

_____

_____

_____

**10.** *Do you think it would be easier to be thankful for the Lord's provision if it fell miraculously from the sky every morning and you only had to gather it each day? Why or why not?*

_____

_____

_____

**11.** *Reread Exodus 16:2–4. Then take two minutes of silence, looking for a sentence, phrase, or even one word that stands out as something God may want you to focus on in your life to help you guard against grumbling. If you're meeting with a group, the leader will keep track of time. At the end of two minutes, share your word or phrase with the group if you wish.*

_____

_____

_____

**12.** *How might your grumbling "leaks" be transformed into an overflow of praise for God's sovereign help and care?*

_____

_____

_____

**13.** *If you're meeting with a group or with a friend, how can they pray for you? If you're using this study on your own, what would you like to say to God right now?*

_____

_____

_____

## Practice

The theme of this week's daily Scripture readings is how to not only guard against grumbling and complaining but also how to overcome it. Read each passage slowly, pausing to think about what is being said. Rather than approaching this as an assignment to complete, think of it as an opportunity to meet with the One who loves you most.

# Day 1

*Read Exodus 17:1–7. This story occurs right after the chapter in Exodus you studied this week, where God sent the miraculous manna to eat. Are you surprised the people so quickly returned to grumbling? Why or why not?*

_____

_____

_____

*How understandable was their grumbling in this situation?*

_____

_____

_____

*Why do you suppose God waited until the people were desperate before He provided water? What can we learn about God from this story?*

_____

_____

_____

*Has God ever waited until you were desperate before He provided for you? Explain.*

_____

_____

_____

To help you turn away discontentment and protect against self-pity, write in a journal or on a separate sheet of paper three things for which you are thankful. Express to God today how grateful you are for the specific, and perhaps even quiet, ways He provides for your needs.

## Day 2

*Read Numbers 13:26–14:9. In this passage, Moses sent twelve men into the Promised Land to survey it. The twelve returned with a unanimous report that the region was as fertile as God had promised—but ten of the twelve said the inhabitants of the land were too strong for the Israelites to overcome. Only Caleb and Joshua insisted that God would empower His people and give them victory. How did the Israelites respond to the surveyors' report?*

_____

_____

_____

*Why weren't the people thankful that God was giving them a land that flowed with milk and honey? What are some indicators that they were carrying around a spirit of self-pity?*

_____

_____

_____

*What did Joshua and Caleb see about the situation that the rest of the people did not? How did Joshua and Caleb's attitude about God shape their assessment?*

_____

_____

_____

*What are you tempted to grumble about today? How can you turn your complaints into praise?*

_____

_____

_____

Tell God today that you completely trust Him to lead you into a good place.

## Day 3

*Read Numbers 14:26–35. In this passage, God responded to the people's grumbling about the difficulties of conquering the Promised Land. What did God decide to do? What do you learn about Him from this response?*

_____

_____

_____

*God made an exception for Caleb and Joshua because they had spoken up in favor of going in to conquer the land. What does it tell you about God that He made this exception?*

_____

_____

_____

*Have you ever faced the negative consequences of self-pity? If so, what happened?*

_____

_____

_____

Today, think about what God has given you to do and how you can respond to this task with trust and gratitude rather than fear and grumbling.

## Day 4

*Read Numbers 17:1–13. This story reveals what happened when the Israelites grumbled about the priesthood of Moses' brother, Aaron. What did God do to show that He had chosen Aaron to be the high priest?*

_____

_____

_____

*How was grumbling against Aaron's leadership really grumbling against God?*

_____

_____

_____

*How did the Israelites respond to the miracle of God (verses 12–13)? Why do you suppose they weren't excited and drawn toward God?*

_____

_____

_____

*What does this show about the people's perceptions of God? How might this scene have been different if the people had developed a thankful attitude rather than one of self-pity?*

_____

_____

_____

As you think about this story, consider your own temptations to grumble. Has this story helped you in any way when it comes to your tendency to complain? If so, how?

# Day 5

*Read Matthew 20:1–16. Jesus told this parable to show how God rewards those who serve Him, whether they begin serving Him as young people and are faithful all their lives, or they come to faith late in life and serve Him for a short time. Why did those who worked in the vineyard from the first hour (verse 11) grumble?*

_____

_____

_____

*Why did the owner of the vineyard reward each worker with the same payment?*

_____

_____

_____

*Do you think the owner was unfair in doing this? Why or why not?*

_____

_____

_____

*Think of the most notorious sinner you know. How would you feel if that person came to faith late in life and was given the same welcome into God's kingdom as you are anticipating?*

_____

_____

_____

If you have accepted Jesus as your Lord and Savior, consider what you can learn from this story about your thankfulness to God for *salvation*. Remembering Christ's sacrifice is a great deterrent to discontentment. Offer a prayer of gratitude to Him.

SESSION 3

The Gift
of God's
Presence

## Welcome

There are so many things for which you can be thankful to God beyond His provision for your needs. Among those blessings might be times when God rescued you from a difficult situation and brought you to a place of safety and security. Remembering experiences like these, when the gift of His Presence was especially clear, will build your trust in Him and remind you of His goodness.

Recalling God's deliverance in past seasons of hardship can encourage you that He will be faithful in the face of any future adversity. This is also a practical way to shift your *inclinations* away from discouragement or doubt anytime life starts to frustrate you or feel ordinary. The more you practice thankfulness, the more the Holy Spirit will heighten gratitude in your heart, drawing you closer and closer to God.

In this session, you will have a chance to reflect on some of your past experiences of rescue and praise God for the impact of His Presence.

## Connect

**1. On a scale of 1 to 5, how would you rate the level of well-being you are currently experiencing?**

| 1 | 2 | 3 | 4 | 5 |
|---|---|---|---|---|

Life is agonizingly hard right now                                        Life is absolutely fabulous right now

**2. How does the rating you gave yourself affect your inclination to be thankful?**

## Experience

*This is the day that I have made!* As you rejoice in this day of life, it will yield up to you precious gifts and beneficial training. Walk with Me along the high road of thanksgiving, and you will find all the delights I have made ready for you.

To protect your thankfulness, you must remember that you reside in a fallen world, where blessings and sorrows intermingle freely. A constant focus on adversity defeats many Christians. They walk through a day that is brimming with beauty and brightness, seeing only the grayness of their thoughts. Neglecting the practice of giving thanks has darkened their minds. How precious are My children who remember to thank Me at all times. They can walk through the darkest days with Joy in their hearts because they know that the Light of My Presence is still shining on them. *Rejoice in this day that I have made*, for I am your steadfast Companion.

—*FROM JESUS CALLING, NOVEMBER 26*

**3. *When you consider that today is the day the Lord has made for you, does it move you toward joy and gratitude, toward resentment or disappointment, or toward a combination of these reactions? Explain your response.***

_____

_____

_____

**4. *Does being reminded of God's Presence with you in this day make it easier for you to be thankful? How does your level of focus on adversity affect your awareness of His Presence?***

_____

_____

_____

Let thankfulness rule in your heart. As you thank Me for blessings in your life, a marvelous thing happens. It is as if *scales fall off your eyes*, enabling you to see more and more of My glorious riches. With your eyes thus opened, you can help yourself to whatever you need from My treasure house. Each time you receive one of My golden gifts, let your thankfulness sing out praises to My Name. "Hallelujahs" are the language of heaven, and they can become the language of your heart.

A life of praise and thankfulness becomes a life filled with miracles. Instead of trying to be in control, you focus on Me and what I am doing. This is the power of praise: centering your entire being in Me. This is how I created you to live, for I made you in My own image. Enjoy abundant life by overflowing with praise and thankfulness.

—FROM JESUS CALLING, *NOVEMBER 27*

**5.** *Consider a time in your life when you experienced what felt like "scales" falling off your eyes (Acts 9:18) so you could see God's glorious riches. How did gratitude play a part?*

_____

_____

_____

**6.** *In what ways might "a life of praise and thankfulness [become] a life filled with miracles"?*

_____

_____

_____

## Discuss

Read aloud the following passage from Psalm 107. In this song, an unknown poet expressed his gratitude to God for rescuing him from a series of misfortunes.

> [1] Give thanks to the LORD, for he is good;
>> his love endures forever.
>
> [2] Let the redeemed of the LORD tell their story—
>> those he redeemed from the hand of the foe,
> [3] those he gathered from the lands,
>> from east and west, from north and south.
>
> [4] Some wandered in desert wastelands,
>> finding no way to a city where they could settle.
> [5] They were hungry and thirsty,
>> and their lives ebbed away.
> [6] Then they cried out to the LORD in their trouble,
>> and he delivered them from their distress.
> [7] He led them by a straight way
>> to a city where they could settle.
> [8] Let them give thanks to the LORD for his unfailing love
>> and his wonderful deeds for mankind,
> [9] for he satisfies the thirsty
>> and fills the hungry with good things.
>
> [10] Some sat in darkness, in utter darkness,
>> prisoners suffering in iron chains,
> [11] because they rebelled against God's commands
>> and despised the plans of the Most High.

<sup>12</sup> So he subjected them to bitter labor;
>	they stumbled, and there was no one to help.
<sup>13</sup> Then they cried to the Lord in their trouble,
>	and he saved them from their distress.
<sup>14</sup> He brought them out of darkness, the utter darkness,
>	and broke away their chains.
<sup>15</sup> Let them give thanks to the Lord for his unfailing love
>	and his wonderful deeds for mankind,
<sup>16</sup> for he breaks down gates of bronze
>	and cuts through bars of iron.

<sup>17</sup> Some became fools through their rebellious ways
>	and suffered affliction because of their iniquities.
<sup>18</sup> They loathed all food
>	and drew near the gates of death.
<sup>19</sup> Then they cried to the Lord in their trouble,
>	and he saved them from their distress.
<sup>20</sup> He sent out his word and healed them;
>	he rescued them from the grave.
<sup>21</sup> Let them give thanks to the Lord for his unfailing love
>	and his wonderful deeds for mankind.
<sup>22</sup> Let them sacrifice thank offerings
>	and tell of his works with songs of joy.

<sup>23</sup> Some went out on the sea in ships;
>	they were merchants on the mighty waters.
<sup>24</sup> They saw the works of the Lord,
>	his wonderful deeds in the deep.
<sup>25</sup> For he spoke and stirred up a tempest
>	that lifted high the waves.

<sup>26</sup> They mounted up to the heavens and went down to the depths;

 in their peril their courage melted away.

<sup>27</sup> They reeled and staggered like drunkards;

 they were at their wits' end.

<sup>28</sup> Then they cried out to the LORD in their trouble,

 and he brought them out of their distress.

<sup>29</sup> He stilled the storm to a whisper;

 the waves of the sea were hushed.

<sup>30</sup> They were glad when it grew calm,

 and he guided them to their desired haven.

<sup>31</sup> Let them give thanks to the LORD for his unfailing love

 and his wonderful deeds for mankind.

<sup>32</sup> Let them exalt him in the assembly of the people

 and praise him in the council of the elders.

*7. In verses 2–3, the writer summarized what all the people mentioned in the psalm have in common: they have been rescued from some form of affliction and gathered to a better place. How is this true for each of the people in the verses below?*

| | |
|---|---|
| verses 4–9 | |
| verses 10–16 | |
| verses 17–22 | |
| verses 23–32 | |

**8.** *A repeated element in this psalm is "Then they cried to the LORD in their trouble, and he saved them from their distress." When have you cried to the Lord in your trouble? How did He save you from your distress?*

---

---

---

## Respond

**9.** *The psalmist urged again and again, "Let them give thanks to the LORD for his unfailing love and his wonderful deeds for mankind." Why is it so important to thank the Lord for His care and deliverance? What is the purpose of remembering Him and reliving your gratitude?*

---

---

---

**10.** *The psalmist wrote, "Let the redeemed of the LORD tell their story" (verse 2). Briefly summarize a story of redemption from your life. Consider sharing it out loud if you are meeting with others.*

---

---

---

**11.** *Read Psalm 107:4–9 again. Then take two minutes of silence, looking for a sentence, phrase, or even one word that stands out as something Jesus may want you to focus on in your life. If you're meeting with a group, the leader will keep track of time. At the end of two minutes, you may share your word or phrase with the group if you wish.*

_____

_____

_____

**12.** *Who in your life needs to hear your story of God's Presence?*

_____

_____

_____

**13.** *If you're meeting with a group or with a friend, how can they pray for you? If you're using this study on your own, what would you like to say to God right now?*

_____

_____

_____

## Practice

The theme of this week's daily Scripture readings is expressing thanks to God for the gift of His Presence with you in both times of blessing and times of difficulty. Read each passage slowly, pausing to think about what is being said. Rather than approaching this

as an assignment to complete, think of it as an opportunity to meet with the One who loves you most.

## Day 1

*Read Deuteronomy 26:1–11. What rite did God want the Israelites to perform each year at the beginning of the harvest season? What do you think the people were meant to learn from giving God the first portion (firstfruits) of their harvest?*

---

---

---

*What do you think the Israelites were meant to learn from telling the story that God commanded them to tell in verses 5–10?*

---

---

---

*How is your story like this story? How is it different?*

---

---

---

*What would be the equivalent for you of offering a portion of your harvest to the Lord each year? What would this specifically look like in your life?*

---
---
---

Thank God today for leading you into a "good land." Make a plan to rejoice with others over the blessings you have received.

## Day 2

*Read Psalm 116:1–7. What is this psalmist's story? In what ways do you identify with him?*

---
---
---

*Perhaps right now you are only partway through this story in your life and the "cords of death" are still entangling you. If so, how do the psalmist's words affect you? Does this passage increase your hope? Does it make you wonder why you're not reaching safety more quickly? Explain.*

---
---
---

*What did the psalmist say to his soul in verse 7? How would you put this into your own words?*

_____

_____

_____

*Why did the psalmist say his soul should be at rest? Is your soul at rest? Why or why not?*

_____

_____

_____

Take some time to offer a prayer of thanks to God based on this psalm. Explain why you love the Lord and how He has answered your cry for mercy.

# Day 3

*Read Psalm 116:8–19. For what was the psalmist thankful? How did he express his gratitude?*

_____

_____

_____

*What would be a modern equivalent of lifting up the "cup of salvation" (verse 13)?*

_____

_____

_____

*What would be a modern equivalent of sacrificing a "thank offering" (verse 17)?*

_____

_____

_____

*What does it mean to "call on the name of the LORD" (verse 17)?*

_____

_____

_____

Between now and tomorrow, make a "thank offering" to God by recalling His past acts of mercy in your life and His closeness in your times of need.

# Day 4

*Read Psalm 118:1–7. Why do you think the psalmist repeated the phrase "his love endures forever" four times? Why is this such an important truth to rehearse and reflect on?*

_____

_____

_____

*For what was this psalmist thankful? How did he express his gratitude?*

_____

_____

*For what are you thankful today? How are you expressing your gratitude?*

_____

_____

_____

*Can you say "his love endures forever" with conviction? Why or why not?*

_____

_____

_____

Today, ask God to open your eyes so you can witness signs of His enduring love for you.

# Day 5

*Read Psalm 118:15–21. For what was the psalmist thankful in these verses?*

_____

_____

_____

*How would you describe his emotions? What key words or phrases stand out to you?*

_____

_____

_____

*How do the psalmist's words compare with your attitude toward God right now?*

_____

_____

_____

*How has God been active in your life during the past week? Where have you seen or felt His nearness?*

_____

_____

_____

Say a prayer of thanksgiving to the Lord today—for He is good!

SESSION 4

Thankful in
Times of Trial

## Welcome

How's your posture? That may seem like an odd question, but spiritually speaking, it's worth thinking about. Do you practice a posture of thankfulness no matter what or who you're up against? Or are you more likely to be grateful only when life is going your way?

Acquiring a habit of thanking God for the good things that happen in your life isn't all that hard. But making it a practice to thank God for your trials, your problems, and the things that distress you comes only with discipline. Yet this is a good discipline to develop—no matter how difficult it may be—for the Bible tells every child of God to count their trials as joyful and to give thanks in all things.

In this session, you will explore the reasons why God gives us this seemingly counterintuitive instruction. You will also strive to begin to develop—or to keep exercising—this posture for yourself.

## Connect

**1. What is one trial you are currently facing? (It could be a physical ailment, a problem at work, a challenge in your family—anything that isn't going the way you wish it would.)**

*2. How have you seen God working in the midst of this trial? What have you been learning from the experience for which you can be grateful?*

_____

_____

_____

## Experience

Make friends with the problems in your life. Though many things feel random and wrong, remember that I am sovereign over everything. *I can fit everything into a pattern for good,* but only to the extent that you trust Me. Every problem can teach you something, transforming you little by little into the masterpiece I created you to be. The very same problem can become a stumbling block over which you fall, if you react with distrust and defiance. The choice is up to you, and you will have to choose many times each day whether to trust Me or defy Me.

The best way to befriend your problems is to thank Me for them. This simple act opens your mind to the possibility of benefits flowing from your difficulties. You can even give persistent problems nicknames, helping you to approach them with familiarity rather than with dread. The next step is to introduce them to Me, enabling Me to embrace them in My loving Presence. I will not necessarily remove your problems, but My wisdom is sufficient to bring good out of every one of them.

—*FROM* JESUS CALLING, *MARCH 5*

**3.** *What are some reasons you should "make friends" with your problems?*

_____

_____

_____

**4.** *Would you say you typically react to problems with trust, defiance, or some other attitude? Think about how you are responding to a current problem in your life. Why are you leaning toward that particular reaction?*

_____

_____

_____

Thank Me for your problems. As soon as your mind gets snagged on a difficulty, bring it to Me with thanksgiving. Then ask Me to show you My way to handle the situation. The very act of thanking Me releases your mind from its negative focus. As you turn your attention to Me, the problem fades in significance and loses its power to trip you up. Together we can deal with the situation, either facing it head-on or putting it aside for later consideration.

Most of the situations that entangle your mind are not today's concerns; you have borrowed them from tomorrow. In this case, I lift the problem out of today and deposit it in the future, where it is veiled from your eyes. In its place I give you My Peace, which flows freely from My Presence.

—*FROM JESUS CALLING, MAY 11*

**5. What role can consistent thanksgiving play in the process of dealing with a problem?**

_____

_____

_____

**6. Think of some of the problems that have been on your mind lately. Would you say these are problems for today or for tomorrow? What should you do if any of them are "borrowed . . . from tomorrow"?**

_____

_____

_____

## Discuss

Read aloud the following passages from James 1 and Philippians 4. Note that the word "perseverance" in James 1:4 refers to the ability to hold up under the stress of your difficult circumstances with a right spiritual posture. The term "gentleness" in Philippians 4:5 refers to the habit of withholding retaliation against those who insult or harm you.

> [2] Consider it pure joy, my brothers and sisters, whenever you face trials of many kinds, [3] because you know that the testing of your faith produces perseverance. [4] Let perseverance finish its work so that you may be mature and complete, not lacking anything. (James 1:2–4)
>
> [4] Rejoice in the Lord always. I will say it again: Rejoice! [5] Let your gentleness be evident to all. The Lord is near. [6] Do not be anxious about anything,

but in every situation, by prayer and petition, with thanksgiving, present your requests to God. [7] And the peace of God, which transcends all understanding, will guard your hearts and your minds in Christ Jesus. (Philippians 4:4–7)

*7. According to James, why especially should the people of God rejoice when facing trials? How easy or hard is that for you to do?*

---

---

---

*8. Notice in Philippians 4:4–7 what Paul told us to do in response to trials. Why is this such an important response?*

---

---

---

## Respond

*9. What is the connection between thanksgiving and peace? What would your response consist of if you left out the rejoicing and the thanksgiving?*

---

---

---

**10.** *Think of the last time you practiced being thankful in your circumstances. What impact did it have on you?*

_____

_____

_____

**11.** *Reread Philippians 4:4–7. Then take two minutes of silence, looking for a sentence, phrase, or even one word that stands out as an adjustment that Jesus may want you to make regarding your "thankfulness posture." If you're meeting with a group, the leader will keep track of time. At the end of two minutes, you may share your word or phrase with the group if you wish.*

_____

_____

_____

**12.** *What ideas do you have for improving your spiritual posture before the next trial comes your way? (Make acting on these ideas a daily priority!)*

_____

_____

_____

**13.** *If you're meeting with a group, how can the members pray for you? If you're using this study on your own, what would you like to say to God right now?*

_____

_____

_____

## Practice

The goal of this week's daily Scripture readings is to inspire you to practice offering thanks to God even in the midst of your trials. Read each passage slowly, pausing to think about what is being said. Rather than approaching this as an assignment to complete, think of it as an opportunity to meet with the One who loves you most.

# Day 1

*Read Romans 5:3–5. How are Paul's words in this passage similar to what James said in James 1:2–4? What additional instructions did Paul give?*

_____

_____

_____

*If you are a Christian, in what ways has God's love been poured out in your heart through the Holy Spirit? How do you know that He is at work in your life?*

_____

_____

_____

*How does the fact that God pours out His love to you in the midst of suffering affect your level of hope? Why do you need this kind of hope when you go through trials?*

_____

_____

_____

*How strong is your perseverance? How strong is your hope? (Think of these as two of the vertebrae that allow you to stand taller in your faith.)*

_____

_____

_____

Today, bring your request to God to build perseverance, character, and hope in your heart.

## Day 2

*Read 1 Peter 4:12–13. According to this passage, why should Christ's followers not be surprised when trials come their way? Why do you think some followers of Jesus are surprised when trials come?*

_____

_____

_____

*How do you respond to Peter's statement that a believer's trials enable him or her to share in Christ's suffering? How would your spiritual posture change if you viewed your trials this way?*

_____

_____

_____

*Why did Peter say Christians can rejoice when they participate in the sufferings of Christ?*

_____

_____

_____

*What is a trial that you need to thank God for right now? How easy is it for you to do this?*

_____

_____

_____

Pause now and ask God to help you rejoice in the midst of whatever you are facing so that you may keep your focus on Him and His glory.

## Day 3

*Read 2 Corinthians 6:4–10. How do trials fit into Paul's picture of the way a servant of God displays his or her faith before the watching world?*

_____

_____

_____

*Why would the way you handle trials as a believer affect the way nonbelievers think about Christ and about Christians in general?*

---

---

---

*How is it possible to be "sorrowful, yet always rejoicing" (verse 10)?*

---

---

---

*What would it look like for you to maintain a posture of rejoicing in the midst of trials?*

---

---

---

Pray that God will help you have Paul's attitude toward trials throughout this day.

# Day 4

*Read 2 Corinthians 4:16–18. What does it mean to "lose heart"?*

---

---

---

*According to this passage, why is it that a Christian need never lose heart?*

_____

_____

_____

*Does it help you to think of your affliction as light and momentary? Why or why not?*

_____

_____

_____

*What is the "unseen" that you fix your eyes on? How does thanksgiving help you do that?*

_____

_____

_____

Don't hesitate to tell God if you are tempted to lose heart. Seek His help in fixing your eyes on what is unseen.

## Day 5

*Read 2 Corinthians 12:9–10. Why did Paul say that he was able to boast of his weaknesses?*

_____

_____

_____

*Why do you suppose God's power is made perfect in weakness? Have you ever experienced God working through you when you were weak? If so, describe that experience.*

_____

_____

_____

_____

_____

*What is God's grace? How would you describe His grace in your life as a believer?*

_____

_____

_____

*What do you think Paul meant when he said, "When I am weak, then I am strong" (verse 10)?*

_____

_____

_____

Ask God to open your eyes today to His grace in the midst of your weakness and need.

SESSION 5

# Count Your Blessings

## Welcome

Have you ever actually tried to count your blessings? If so, how far did you get before you lost track of the number?

For starters, God provides for your physical needs: the food you eat, the water you drink, the roof over your head. He provides the air you breathe and the ground on which you walk. He provides you with family, friends, education, and work. Most important of all, He tends to your *spiritual* needs. His Son, Jesus, paid a great cost to meet the deepest needs of your soul. When you recognize with gratitude—not just on Sundays or religious holidays but in your day-to-day life—*everything* He has done, you can be more patient about your as-yet-unfulfilled desires for this world.

In this session, your gratitude is bound to multiply as you look at some of the innumerable ways that God has responded to your spiritual needs. Though it's humanly impossible to count His infinite blessings, that shouldn't prevent you from trying! As the author of Psalm 103:1–2 encouraged, "Praise the Lord, my soul; all my inmost being, praise his holy name. Praise the Lord, my soul, and forget not all his benefits."

## Connect

**1.** *How would you describe the spiritual blessings that God has given to you?*

_____

_____

_____

**2.** *If you have accepted Jesus as your Savior, when were you first aware of the depths of God's mercy toward you in rescuing you from your sin? How did your story of faith begin?*

_____

_____

_____

## Experience

Rest in My Presence, allowing Me to take charge of this day. Do not bolt into the day like a racehorse suddenly released. Instead, walk purposefully with Me, letting Me direct your course one step at a time. Thank Me for each blessing along the way; this brings Joy to both you and Me. A grateful heart protects you from negative thinking. Thankfulness enables you to see the abundance I shower upon you daily. Your prayers and petitions are winged into heaven's throne room when they are permeated with thanksgiving. *In everything give thanks, for this is My will for you.*

—*FROM* JESUS CALLING, *FEBRUARY 25*

**3.** *How does thanking God "for each blessing along the way" encourage the habit of letting Him be in charge of your day?*

_____

_____

_____

**4.** *How does a grateful heart protect you from negative thinking?*

_____

_____

_____

Thank Me frequently as you journey through today. This practice makes it possible to *pray without ceasing*, as the apostle Paul taught. If you are serious about learning to pray continually, the best approach is to thank Me in every situation. These thankful prayers provide a solid foundation on which you can build all your other prayers. Moreover, a grateful attitude makes it easier for you to communicate with Me.

When your mind is occupied with thanking Me, you have no time for worrying or complaining. If you practice thankfulness consistently, negative thought patterns will gradually grow weaker and weaker. *Draw near to Me* with a grateful heart, and My Presence will *fill you with Joy and Peace.*

—FROM JESUS CALLING, NOVEMBER 25

**5.** *What are some of the benefits of purposefully thanking God in every situation?*

_____

_____

_____

**6. *Do you have any negative thought patterns that you would like to have weakened by a habit of thankful thoughts? If so, what are those patterns?***

_____

_____

_____

## Discuss

Read aloud the following passage from Ephesians 1. Note that "every spiritual blessing" (verse 3) means blessings received through connection with the Spirit of God (verses 13–14). "Redemption" (verse 7) means buying back someone or something—such as buying a person out of slavery. Furthermore, Paul used the male noun in the phrase "adoption to sonship" (verse 5) to indicate that all who welcome Christ into their lives are welcomed into a family relationship with God, with the full rights that Roman law gave to adult sons who were heirs.

> [3] Praise be to the God and Father of our Lord Jesus Christ, who has blessed us in the heavenly realms with every spiritual blessing in Christ. [4] For he chose us in him before the creation of the world to be holy and blameless in his sight. In love [5] he predestined us for adoption to sonship through Jesus Christ, in accordance with his pleasure and will—[6] to the praise of his glorious grace, which he has freely given us in the One he loves. [7] In him we have redemption through his blood, the forgiveness of sins, in accordance with the riches of God's grace [8] that he lavished on us. With all wisdom and understanding, [9] he made known to us the mystery of his will according to his good pleasure, which he purposed in Christ, [10] to be put into effect when the times reach their fulfillment—to bring unity to all things in heaven and on earth under Christ.

<sup>11</sup> In him we were also chosen, having been predestined according to the plan of him who works out everything in conformity with the purpose of his will, <sup>12</sup> in order that we, who were the first to put our hope in Christ, might be for the praise of his glory. <sup>13</sup> And you also were included in Christ when you heard the message of truth, the gospel of your salvation. When you believed, you were marked in him with a seal, the promised Holy Spirit, <sup>14</sup> who is a deposit guaranteeing our inheritance until the redemption of those who are God's possession—to the praise of his glory.

*7. Review some of the spiritual blessings from this passage that Paul said have been afforded to every believer:*

- being chosen to become holy and blameless

- being adopted into God's family with the full rights of a son and heir

- being redeemed out of slavery by Christ's blood

- receiving God's grace as He lavishly gives Himself to you

- receiving forgiveness of sins

- being given God's plan to unify all things

- receiving the Holy Spirit inside you, who makes every other blessing possible

*Which of these stand out to you? How easy is it for you to recount with thankfulness the things that God has done for you? Why is it often easy to overlook these blessings?*

**8.** *Paul repeated the phrase "the praise of his glory" in this passage. God's "glory" is the revelation of who He truly is, and when that is revealed, praise naturally follows. What can you learn about God from this passage that will lead you to ever-increasing thanksgiving and praise?*

_____

_____

_____

## Respond

**9.** *As a believer, God has blessed you in Christ, chosen you in Christ, and adopted you through Christ. To be "in Christ" is to be connected to Him, drawing your very life from Him. Why should you be thankful for being "in Christ"?*

_____

_____

_____

**10.** *What would help you become more deeply thankful for being chosen and adopted into God's family, bought out of slavery, and brought into intimate connection with Christ?*

_____

_____

_____

**11.** *Reread the passage out loud. Then take two minutes of silence, looking for a sentence, phrase, or even one word that stands out as something Jesus may want you to focus on in order to more consistently count your blessings. If you're meeting with a group, the leader will keep track of time. At the end of two minutes, you may share your word or phrase with the group if you wish.*

_____

_____

_____

**12.** *What are some additional spiritual blessings you can think of that you've never counted before? What practical blessings would you add to that list?*

_____

_____

_____

**13.** *If you're meeting with a group or with a friend, how can they pray for you? If you're using this study on your own, what would you like to say to God right now?*

_____

_____

_____

## Practice

The theme of this week's daily Scripture readings is remembering to thank God for the spiritual blessings that He has supplied. Read each passage slowly, pausing to think about what is being said. Rather than approaching this as an assignment to complete, think of it as an opportunity to meet with the One who loves you most.

# Day 1

*Read Colossians 1:12–14. For what did Paul urge the people of God to give thanks to the Father?*

_____

_____

_____

*What is the "kingdom of light"? What do you know about it?*

_____

_____

_____

_____

*What is the "dominion of darkness"? Why should Christians be thankful to be rescued from it?*

_____

_____

_____

*How thankful are you for this rescue? What helps you to be thankful? What gets in the way?*

---
---
---

Today, talk with God about the amazing thing He has done for you by including you in the kingdom of light.

## Day 2

*Read Ephesians 1:18–20. In this passage, Paul prayed that the eyes of the believers' hearts "may be enlightened." How would this promote your gratitude to God?*

---
---
---
---

*What is the hope to which God has called you as a disciple of Christ? Why should you be thankful for that hope?*

---
---
---

*What is the "inheritance" that God has waiting for His children? How should this impact your sense of gratitude today?*

_____

_____

_____

*How did Paul describe the power at work on a believer's behalf? In what ways is this a blessing in your life?*

_____

_____

_____

Choose one item from this passage and pour out your thankfulness about it to God.

## Day 3

*Read Ephesians 2:1–10. How would you describe the condition of those who are spiritually dead? What does it mean to be "alive with Christ" (verse 5)?*

_____

_____

_____

*What is so important about believers being seated with Christ in the heavenly realms (verse 6)? Pause to reflect on this, and then explain why it makes you thankful.*

_____

_____

_____

*What is the connection between grace (verses 5, 8) and gratitude?*

_____

_____

_____

*How will you express your gratitude to God for His grace in your life?*

_____

_____

_____

Thank God today for rescuing you from the bondage to "the ruler of the kingdom of the air" (verse 2).

# Day 4

*Read Hebrews 12:28–29. What does it mean that God's kingdom "cannot be shaken"?*

_____

_____

_____

*What else do you know about God's kingdom? Why should you be thankful for it?*

_____

_____

_____

*Why does God deserve to be worshiped with reverence and awe?*

_____

_____

_____

*What does picturing God as "a consuming fire" (verse 29) reveal about Him? When you think of Him in this way, does it inspire you to gratitude? Why or why not?*

_____

_____

_____

Approach God with awe today, expressing thanks that He has made it possible for every believer to safely and intimately approach Him.

## Day 5

*Read Colossians 4:2–6. What is watchfulness in prayer? Why is it important?*

_____

_____

_____

*How does watchfulness in prayer go along with thankfulness in prayer?*

_____

_____

_____

*The "mystery of Christ" (verse 3) is the revealed secret that Christ has come to dwell in the Gentiles and not just the Jews. Why is that something for which you can be thankful?*

_____

_____

_____

*How thankful are you for the wonder of what God has done in Christ? What would help you grow in your gratitude for that?*

_____

_____

_____

Pour out your thanks to God in this moment for His countless spiritual blessings.

SESSION 6

# Celebrating
# Your Life
# in Christ

## Welcome

Jesus died to pay for your sins, and He rose from the dead as evidence that the price was paid in full. His resurrection triumphantly declared that He had conquered death once and for all and that His followers would likewise one day rise to life again after their own deaths.

What a miracle and blessing this is! Jesus' resurrection made it possible for *anyone* to die to sin and live a new life in intimate relationship with Him. In fact, His resurrection accomplished so much good that His followers still celebrate it every Sunday. But how about keeping the celebration going? If you call on Jesus as the way, the truth, and the life, you have the wondrous privilege of getting to rejoice in Him *every single day*.

In this session, you will reflect on the resurrection, seeking to expand on your thankfulness for this most amazing event and for the life you have in Christ—both now and for eternity.

## Connect

**1.** *Why is it important that Jesus not only died for humanity's sin but also rose from the grave?*

_____

_____

_____

_____

**2. What are some ways (outside of Easter events) that you and your church celebrate the resurrection?**

_____

_____

_____

## Experience

Draw near to Me with a thankful heart, aware that your cup is overflowing with blessings. Gratitude enables you to perceive Me more clearly and to rejoice in our Love-relationship. *Nothing can separate you from My loving Presence!* That is the basis of your security. Whenever you start to feel anxious, remind yourself that your security rests in Me alone, and I am totally trustworthy.

You will never be in control of your life circumstances, but you can relax and trust in My control. Instead of striving for a predictable, safe lifestyle, seek to know Me in greater depth and breadth. I long to make your life a glorious adventure, but you must stop clinging to old ways. I am always doing something new within My beloved ones. Be on the lookout for all that I have prepared for you.

—*FROM JESUS CALLING, JULY 5*

**3. Why do you suppose gratitude helps you perceive Jesus more clearly?**

_____

_____

**4.** *As a believer, how easy is it for you to relax and trust in Jesus' control of your situation? What helps you do that? What gets in the way?*

_____

_____

_____

Come to Me for all that you need. Come into My Presence with thanksgiving, for thankfulness opens the door to My treasures. When you are thankful, you affirm the central truth that I am Good. I am Light, in *whom there is no darkness at all.* The assurance that I am entirely Good meets your basic need for security. Your life is not subject to the whims of a sin-stained deity.

Relax in the knowledge that the One who controls your life is totally trustworthy. Come to Me with confident expectation. There is nothing you need that I cannot provide.

—FROM JESUS CALLING, MAY 5

**5.** *Why is it so important to be convinced that God is good?*

_____

_____

_____

**6.** *What evidence do you have that the One who controls your life is completely trustworthy? How is the resurrection evidence of Jesus' trustworthiness?*

_____

_____

_____

## Discuss

Read aloud the following passage from 1 Corinthians 15. Here, Paul explained some of the meaning of the resurrection for those who believe in Christ. As you read, note that "firstfruits" (verses 20, 23) refers to the first portion of a harvest, while "dominion, authority and power" (verse 24) refers to demonic powers.

> [14] If Christ has not been raised, our preaching is useless and so is your faith. [15] More than that, we are then found to be false witnesses about God, for we have testified about God that he raised Christ from the dead. . . . [17] And if Christ has not been raised, your faith is futile; you are still in your sins. [18] Then those also who have fallen asleep in Christ are lost. [19] If only for this life we have hope in Christ, we are of all people most to be pitied.
>
> [20] But Christ has indeed been raised from the dead, the firstfruits of those who have fallen asleep. [21] For since death came through a man, the resurrection of the dead comes also through a man. [22] For as in Adam all die, so in Christ all will be made alive. [23] But each in turn: Christ, the firstfruits; then, when he comes, those who belong to him. [24] Then the end will come, when he hands over the kingdom to God the Father after he has destroyed all dominion, authority and power.

*7. Why is the Christian faith futile without the resurrection (verse 17)? What would life look like for every follower of Christ if the resurrection hadn't happened?*

_____

_____

_____

_____

**8.** *Why did Paul say, "If only for this life we have hope in Christ, we are of all people most to be pitied" (verse 19)? Why are those who have this type of "hope" to be pitied?*

_____

_____

_____

## Respond

**9.** *Why was it necessary for Christ to be "the firstfruits of those who have fallen asleep" (verse 20)?*

_____

_____

_____

**10.** *Because Christ was raised from the dead, believers can look forward to rising to life again after they die. They are destined for a new heaven and a new earth (Revelation 21). How do you imagine your ultimate destiny? How attractive to you is that picture?*

_____

_____

_____

_____

**11.** *Reread 1 Corinthians 15:14–19. Then take two minutes of silence, looking for a sentence, phrase, or even one word that Jesus may be using to invite you to greater joy in Him. If you're meeting with a group, the leader will keep track of time. At the end of two minutes, you may share your word or phrase with the group if you wish.*

**12.** *What are some ways that you could begin to celebrate Christ's resurrection in your everyday life?*

**13.** *If you're meeting with a group, how can the members pray for you? If you're using this study on your own, what would you like to say to God right now?*

## Practice

The theme of this week's daily Scripture reading is to help you contemplate and further rejoice in Jesus' resurrection. Read each passage slowly, pausing to think about what is being said. Rather than approaching this as an assignment to complete, think of it as an opportunity to meet with the One who loves you most.

# Day 1

*Read Luke 24:1–8. Imagine being one of the women going to the tomb. What do you see? What do you hear? What do you feel?*

_____

_____

_____

*Why do you suppose the women didn't expect Jesus' resurrection, even though He had promised it?*

_____

_____

_____

*Why weren't these women immediately thankful?*

_____

_____

_____

*How does this story affect you now? How easy is it for you to get to a place of wonder and gratitude for this event? Explain.*

Today, go to God with your honest response to Jesus' resurrection.

## Day 2

*Read Romans 6:4–11. If you are a believer in Christ, how have you already experienced death and resurrection with Him?*

*What has been your experience of new life in Jesus? What impact does it have on your life knowing Jesus has conquered death?*

*In what ways is your death and resurrection yet to come?*

_____

_____

_____

*Living in light of the fact that Jesus has defeated death means being dead to sin. What does that involve? How can you count yourself dead to sin this week?*

_____

_____

_____

Seek God's help in counting yourself "dead to sin."

# Day 3

*Read Luke 24:36–49. Imagine yourself as one of the people in this scene. What do you see? What do you hear? What do you feel? What do you do?*

_____

_____

_____

*How did Jesus prove that He wasn't a ghost? What understanding about the nature of a resurrected body do you gain from this account?*

---

---

---

*What was the point of Jesus showing His followers His hands and feet (verse 40)? Imagine seeing those hands and feet. How do you respond?*

---

---

---

Share with God today your gratitude that Jesus' resurrected hands and feet still show the scars of His crucifixion.

## Day 4

*Read Colossians 2:9–15. Why did Paul describe baptism as a burial (verse 12)? How is baptism also a resurrection?*

---

---

---

*How did Paul describe what God has done for His children in verses 13–14? How does the resurrection put the demonic powers to shame?*

_____

_____

_____

*What are you celebrating as you read this passage? List as many things as possible.*

_____

_____

_____

_____

*Why are you thankful for those things you listed? How do they make a difference to your life here and now?*

_____

_____

_____

Offer thanks and praise to God for what He has done for you through Jesus' death and resurrection.

# Day 5

*Read Matthew 28:1–10. How is Matthew's version of Jesus' resurrection similar to Luke's account in Luke 24:1–8? How is it different?*

-----------------------------------------------------------------------

-----------------------------------------------------------------------

-----------------------------------------------------------------------

*What additional information do you learn from Matthew's account?*

-----------------------------------------------------------------------

-----------------------------------------------------------------------

-----------------------------------------------------------------------

*The angel rolled the stone away from the mouth of the tomb not to let Jesus out (He was already gone) but to show the women that He had risen. Why was it important for them to see the empty tomb? Why was it necessary for the angel to tell the women not to be afraid?*

-----------------------------------------------------------------------

-----------------------------------------------------------------------

-----------------------------------------------------------------------

*Would you have been afraid if this happened to you? Why or why not?*

-----------------------------------------------------------------------

-----------------------------------------------------------------------

-----------------------------------------------------------------------

Express to God what you're thankful for today as you read this story.

In Romans 10:9, Paul wrote, "If you declare with your mouth, 'Jesus is Lord,' and believe in your heart that God raised him from the dead, you will be saved." As you conclude this study, thank God for giving you the incredible offer of salvation, for His loving Presence and provision in your life, for allowing you to be part of His work on this earth as a follower of Christ, and for the ways He has helped and will continue to help you not only *be* thankful but *practice thankfulness* through the power of the Holy Spirit.

# Leader's Notes

Thank you for your willingness to lead a group through this *Jesus Calling* study on practicing thankfulness. The rewards of leading are different from the rewards of participating, and we hope you find your own walk with Jesus deepened by this experience. In many ways, your group meetings will be structured like other Bible studies in which you've participated. You'll want to open in prayer, for example, and ask people to silence their phones. These leader's notes will focus on elements of the study that may be new to you.

## Welcome

This first portion of the study is intended as an engaging introduction into the overall theme of the session. It is purposefully brief to allow plenty of time for group interaction during the meeting.

## Connect

This segment functions as an icebreaker. It gets the group members thinking about the topic at hand by asking them to share from their own experience. Some people may be tempted to tell a long story in response to one of these questions, but the goal is to keep the answers brief. Ideally, you want everyone in the group to have a chance to answer the *Connect* questions, so you may want to explain up front that everyone needs to limit his or her answer to one minute and consider keeping track of the time for them.

With the rest of the study, it is generally not a good idea to go around the circle and have everyone answer every question—a free-flowing discussion is more desirable. But with the *Connect* questions, each person's participation is preferred. Encourage those who are shy to share, but don't force them. Tell the group that anyone should feel free to pass if they prefer not to answer a question.

## Experience

This is the group's chance to talk about excerpts from the *Jesus Calling* devotional. You will need to monitor this discussion closely so that you have enough time for the actual study of God's Word that follows. If the group gets involved in a long and rich discussion on one of the devotional excerpts, you may choose to skip the other one and move on to the Bible study. Don't feel obliged to cover every *Experience* question if the current conversation is fruitful. On the other hand, do move on if the group gets off on a tangent or is only minimally responsive to a question.

## Discuss

This is the place where the deeper biblical study about living thankfully begins. Each *Discuss* section opens with one or more Bible passages that the group can read aloud. Next, two questions are presented to get everyone thinking about the meaning of what they've just read. This material will prepare people's minds and hearts for the lengthier response section that follows.

## Respond

Try to do the *Respond* exercise in session 1 on your own before the group meets the first time so you can coach people on what to expect—and remember to complete each

session's *Respond* portion in advance of each meeting that follows. Your preparation is something the Holy Spirit will use to serve the teaching and conversation.

Note that this section may be a little different from Bible studies your group has done in the past. After the group's discussion about the meaning of the Bible passage, ample opportunities are provided in the various *Respond* questions to go deeper scripturally and to begin to apply the insights gained from God's Word. But the unique aspect of this study is the time of silence after the group rereads the specified scripture. Everyone will have a chance to pray about what God might want to say to them personally through the reading—how they can be more thankful and exercise that gratitude more often. It will be up to you to keep track of the two minutes and to call people back together when the time is up. (Choose a gentle chime or other pleasant timer sound on your phone instead of a disruptive noise.) If the group members aren't used to being silent in a "crowd," brief them on what to expect.

Don't be afraid to let people sit in silence. Two minutes of quiet may seem like a long time at first, but it will help to train group members to sit in silence with God when they are alone. They can remain where they are in the circle, or if you have space, you can let them go by themselves to other rooms at your instruction. If your group meets in a home, ask the host before the meeting starts about which rooms are available for use. Some people will be more comfortable in the quiet if they have a bit of space from others. Start the two minutes once everyone is situated and ready.

When everyone reconvenes after the time of silence, invite them to share what they experienced. There are several questions provided in this study guide that you can ask. Note that it's not necessary to cover every question if the group has a good discussion going. It's also not necessary to go around the circle and make everyone share.

Don't be concerned if some individuals are reserved and slow to speak up after the exercise. People are often quiet when they are pulling together their ideas, and the exercise will have been a new experience for many of them. Just ask a question and let it hang in the air until someone answers. You can then say, "Thank you. What about others? What came to you when you sat with the passage?"

If anyone says they found it hard to quiet their minds enough to focus on the passage for those few minutes, tell them this is okay; they're practicing a skill, and

sometimes skills take time to learn. As they learn to sit quietly with God's Word in a group, they will become much more comfortable sitting with the Word on their own. Remind them that spending time in the Bible each day is one of the most valuable things they can do as believers in Christ.

## Practice

It's not necessary for group members to prepare anything for the study ahead of time. However, at the end of each study are five days' worth of suggestions for spending time in God's Word and putting the session's theme into action during the next week. These daily times are optional but valuable, so encourage the group to do them. Also, invite them to bring their questions and insights to the group at your next meeting, especially if they had a breakthrough moment or if they didn't understand something.

## Preparing for Group Time

As the leader, there are a few things you should do to prepare for each meeting:

- *Read through the session.* This will help you become familiar with the content and know how to structure the discussion times.
- *Spend five to ten minutes doing the* Discuss *and* Respond *questions on your own.* When the group meets, you'll be watching the clock, so you'll probably have a more fulfilling time with the passage if you do these two exercises beforehand. You can then spend time in the passage again with the group. This way, you'll be sure to have the key verses for that session deeply in your mind.
- *Pray for your group.* Pray especially that God will guide them into a deeper understanding of how they can be thankful to Him in every area of life.
- *Bring extra supplies to your meeting.* Group members should bring their own pens for writing notes and answering the Bible reflection, but it's a good idea to have

extras available for those who forget. You may also want to bring paper and Bibles for those who may have neglected to bring their study guides to the meeting.

Following you will find suggested answers for some of the study questions. Note that in many cases there is no one right answer, especially when group members are sharing their personal experiences.

## Session 1: Open Your Eyes to God's Abundance

1. *Answers will vary. The goal here is to get people thinking about thankfulness and opening up to each other about the topic of seeing God's abundance all around them.*

2. *Some people have a harder time noticing good things than others do. It's less a matter of how much hardship a person faces than it is a matter of attitude. Some people are naturally more attuned to negative input than positive input. The goal of this entire study is to help group members recognize God's infinite blessings and practice thankfulness more and more.*

3. *Eve focused on the one fruit she couldn't have—as if she was somehow lacking God's abundance—rather than being thankful for the bountiful garden He had made freely available to her.*

4. *When we focus on what we don't have or on what we're displeased about, our minds become "darkened" like Eve's. We take for granted the countless gifts of God. We look for what is wrong and refuse to enjoy life until the negative things are "fixed." We're also more likely to resent God and try to get our own way because we see Him as stingy.*

5. *Answers will vary, but here's a key point: acknowledging that all we have and all we are belongs to God can inspire our gratitude and help us see our need to be truly grateful for His generosity. Think of it: He freely lets us use and enjoy the resources He has provided, and He does it because He loves us! On the other hand, if we think those things belong to us, we're less likely to see them as gifts for which to be thankful.*

**6.** *Answers will vary.*

7. *Satan claimed that if Eve ate the fruit, she would be like God, knowing good and evil. However, when she and Adam actually ate the fruit, they only felt shame and wanted to cover themselves. In addition, Satan said Adam and Eve wouldn't die if they ate the fruit, but they did die spiritually the moment they sinned—and the process began that would lead eventually to their physical deaths.*

8. *Eve could have thought something like this: God has provided abundantly for my need for food. I am so grateful for His provision and for the privilege of being intimate with Him that I will obey His command about this one tree, even though I don't understand the reason for it. This fruit is appealing, but there's so much more! As I look around, I see a world of things to be thankful for! The Lord has given me life, He has given me Adam, and He has given me this beautiful garden. I can trust Him to provide for me in all ways and be sure that He will withhold nothing good.*

**9.** *Among the many possibilities, some examples could include physical pain, not enough money, a job we don't like, or a relationship we don't have.*

**10.** *Answers will vary.*

**11.** *Answers will vary. Be sure to keep track of time (two minutes).*

*It's fine for this process to be unfamiliar to the group members at first. Note that some people may find the silence intimidating initially. Their anxiety might tempt them to fill the air with noise, but it will be helpful for these group members to just take a quiet moment before God. Let them express their discomfort once you're all gathered together again, but make sure it is balanced by those who found the silence strengthening. Helping people become comfortable with this "holy quiet" will serve their private daily times with God in wonderful ways.*

**12.** *Answers will vary.*

13. *Responses will vary. Take as much time as you can to pray for each other. You might have someone write down the requests so you can keep track of answers to prayer at future group meetings.*

## Session 2: Guarding Against Grumbling

1. *Some examples could include being agitated or upset that we don't have all the things our friends or neighbors have; wishing our lives looked more like the other "perfect" families we know; or acting out these feelings by grumbling, complaining, or being rude to others.*

2. *Answers will vary, but most likely, feelings of self-pity will arise when we compare ourselves to others and decide we don't measure up, when we feel we are being treated unfairly, or when trial or tragedy comes our way and we can't understand why we have to go through it.*

3. *Self-pity is like a pit with crumbling edges: once we start feeling sorry for ourselves, we slide deeper and deeper into this negative hole—and it only gets harder to climb back out to a place of contentment. Anytime that Christians get stuck in self-pity, it ultimately saps our relationship with God and with other people, leaving us feeling isolated.*

4. *Being thankful to God each day magnifies the good things that are happening. These things loom larger in our eyes, and what we lack appears smaller. The habit of thankfulness also opens us to His Presence, which offers protection from many negative states, including self-pity, and from the lure of temptation.*

5. *Answers will vary. With our grumbling, we are basically saying the world isn't going the way it should—according to us. It's okay to feel sadness when life doesn't follow our plan, but grumbling goes beyond disappointment to actively challenging God's design and infinite knowledge as the Sovereign of the universe. It also causes us to doubt God's provision in our lives.*

**6.** *When you perceive life through a grid of gratitude, you can look at a difficult day at work, for example, and say, "Thank You, Jesus, for providing me with the strength to handle these challenges, just as You've provided a way through these kinds of obstacles in the past." You see the situation as manageable because you are viewing it with different eyes.*

**7.** *The Israelites now remembered Egypt as a place where they ate as much as they wanted, including meat. It's possible they did eat meat in Egypt, but as slaves they probably ate mostly bread—and not necessarily all they wanted. They were glamorizing the past while conveniently forgetting the suffering they had faced and how much they had complained to God about their plight at the time.*

**8.** *Answers will vary. Try to think of something in your own life that you're tempted to complain about, and be ready to share it with the group if others are slow to answer.*

**9.** *The Lord gave the people quail one evening, and after that He gave them manna every day—though just enough for that day. The people didn't have extra, but they did have enough for their needs. Some beyond-the-surface answers include: God heard their desires, not just their needs. He was willing to reveal His glory to the Israelites again, after all the things He had already miraculously done for them. He gave the manna a sweet flavor; it wasn't tasteless.*

**10.** *Some group members may say yes, it would be easier, because the provision would so obviously be from God and not from their own hard labor. Others may say no, it wouldn't be easier, because getting the same manna day after day would get boring—and sinful hearts would be tempted to grumble about it. The key is that grumbling is in the heart of the grumbler, and he or she will find something to complain about no matter the situation.*

**11.** *Answers will vary.*

**12.** *Answers will vary.*

**13.** *Responses will vary.*

# Session 3: The Gift of God's Presence

**1.** *As group members respond, take note of those who rate their lives at a 1 or 2, and plan to pray for them at the end of your meeting.*

**2.** *It is certainly more difficult to be thankful when we rate our lives more toward "agonizingly hard" than "absolutely fabulous." However, even in seasons of adversity, there is always something for which we can be thankful.*

**3.** *Whereas questions 1 and 2 asked about life in general, this one drills down specifically to your group members' lives today. If they can be thankful for this day, even with all its flaws, they are making progress. Still, your meetings should be a safe place for people to admit their tendency toward resentment or disappointment, because they can't grow if they feel they have to hide the truth.*

**4.** *Focusing on adversity actually hinders our awareness of God's Presence, while remembering His Presence magnifies His work in our lives. As we make the choice to be thankful for this gift, it kick-starts this upward cycle.*

**5.** *Answers will vary. One example of "scales" falling from a person's eyes could be seeing a situation in a new light: discovering how God really was there in a situation and understanding the protection and deliverance He provided at that time. Gratitude always plays a part in this process because it helps us focus on something other than ourselves and our own problems—which in turn allows us to see the situation from a different perspective.*

**6.** *Living a life of praise and thankfulness opens our eyes to the miracles God is doing around us every day that we might have previously overlooked. We are more likely to make positive choices, treat others with love and kindness, and look for ways to bless them— which will lead to healthier relationships. A life of praise and thankfulness also positions us to receive other blessings from God, even healings and restorations. God doesn't guarantee everything will go our way if we are thankful, but we will more readily expect good things to happen as we focus on Him and all that He is doing.*

7. *Psalm 107:4–9 describes the homeless getting homes and being rescued from hunger and thirst. Verses 10–16 speak of prisoners doing hard labor being set free. Verses 17–22 describe people who became sick because of their sin, and when they turned back to God, He healed them. Verses 23–32 speak of rescue from shipwreck at sea.*

8. *Answers will vary, but you might want to have the group share some stories of rescue to encourage one another. The Lord doesn't always make everything instantly better, as the end of this psalm makes clear. Sometimes He allows our suffering to last much longer than we wish, and sometimes He allows tragedies to happen that will never be fixed in this life. But He often rescues us in our difficulties—and He is ever faithful to save His followers eternally.*

9. *We build these habits so that the next time we face hardship, we have a strong memory of God's closeness, His character, and His power. Remembering Him will help to carry us through the new hard place. When things aren't going well, negative feelings can easily overwhelm us. A list of loving rescues to rehearse can counteract this.*

10. *Allow group members to briefly tell their stories of redemption from sin or from some experience of suffering. It's important for each of us to call to mind these narratives because they reinforce our gratitude and motivate others to think of their own redemption stories. Those who hear our "good reports" will also be more likely to recognize God's love and kindness in their particular situations and realize their need to be thankful. Sharing these stories helps others know us better, too, which strengthens the bonds of friendship.*

11. *Answers will vary.*

12. *Answers will vary.*

13. *Responses will vary.*

# Session 4: Thankful in Times of Trial

**1.** *Allow a few minutes for the group members to share their trials.*

**2.** *Answers will vary.*

**3.** *Every problem we face can either help transform us into the masterpiece God intended or become a stumbling block that hinders us. When we "make friends" with our problems, we see them in a different light, recognizing that God is truly in control of all that happens. Rather than striving to fix everything ourselves, we rely on the power of God—and this teaches us to trust in Him.*

**4.** *Once again, make your group a safe place for people to admit their struggles. Encourage them to consider what "defiance" looks like in their lives (complaining, anger, bargaining). While it may take time for them to get to the point of trusting God on any given issue, it's good for them to be aware of where they are in the process.*

**5.** *As soon as we realize that our minds are chewing on a difficulty, we should go to God in prayer and thank Him for His promise to never leave us on our own during a time of trial (Hebrews 13:5). We should also consistently express our gratitude as He reveals the ways He is (and has already been) working on our behalf, as He shows us the course to take to handle the situation, and as He brings us to a place of resolution. The thanksgiving must always come first, because this affects how our minds respond to the difficulty and how receptive we are to God's guidance.*

**6.** *Answers will vary. For many of the challenges we face, some advance planning is needed—the reading is not intended to encourage procrastination. However, it's important for us not to worry about the things we cannot solve ahead of time. If we do find ourselves borrowing problems from tomorrow, we should acknowledge that things are out of our control and leave those issues in God's hands. This readies us to get to work when God calls us to step back into the situation and take action.*

7. *James said we should rejoice when we face trials because having our faith tested leads to perseverance, which is the habit of continuing to work at something even when it is hard. Perseverance, in turn, is a key component of spiritual maturity. We will struggle to thank God for our trials until we develop a habit of doing so in the midst of suffering.*

8. *Paul agreed with James that we should rejoice in God always, including when we face trials. He said we should respond to trials with gentleness and with thankful, prayerful petitions to God. This means choosing faith over the fret of anxiety, and in those times when others are insulting or harming us, choosing not to retaliate even when we could do so. According to Scripture, such trust puts us in a position of strength, not weakness.*

9. *Thanksgiving leads us to involve God in the process and recognize He is in control. If we don't have to be in charge, we don't have to carry all the burdens that come with it. A response without thanksgiving would be heavy with desperate requests for God to rescue us from the trial. There would be a thread of anxiety running through our prayers, making it harder to pray in faith. Thanksgiving is crucial for "cleaning out" the faithless anxiety from our prayers.*

10. *Answers will vary. It may be useful to explain the difference between thankful in and thankful for. God doesn't expect us to thank Him for evil, but we can thank Him for the good that He sovereignly brings out of it. Also keep in mind that there may be some in the group who have never practiced being thankful in their circumstances. Compassionately acknowledge this and invite them to share what may have prevented this. Then encourage them that God stands ready to help them start writing new chapters with Him in their faith journey.*

11. *Answers will vary.*

12. *Answers will vary.*

13. *Responses will vary.*

# Session 5: Count Your Blessings

1. *Answers will vary, but every person who has repented of their sins and accepted God's gift of salvation can certainly claim the blessings of knowing their sins are forgiven and having a place reserved for them in heaven (John 14:2–3).*

2. *While there won't be time for people to tell their entire testimony, they can tell how old they were when they became aware of God's mercy and share a few of the circumstances surrounding their coming to faith in Christ.*

3. *When we lead a life of thankfulness, we walk purposefully through the day, allowing God to direct our course one step at a time. Thankfulness says that all things—whether they seem good or bad—are sifted through the hands of a loving and sovereign God.*

4. *Instead of choosing to pay attention to the negative things that happen, a grateful heart chooses to pay attention to the positives. Negative things simply don't register as strongly, and our mood isn't as affected by them. We don't drift into thought patterns where we're imagining worst-case scenarios over and over but instead remain in a state of trusting in God for the outcome.*

5. *Some possible answers: Purposefully thanking God in every situation helps us develop the habit of praying without ceasing, which Paul urged in 1 Thessalonians 5:16–18. It's a biblical way to avoid giving Satan an easy opportunity at our hearts and minds (Ephesians 4:27). Thanking God also crowds out worrying and complaining. It is impossible to think anxious thoughts and thankful thoughts at the same time.*

6. *Answers will vary but might include patterns such as habitual worry, complaining, impulsiveness, selfishness, or self-criticism.*

7. *Examples of answers could include: "I'm thankful for being adopted into God's family, because I long for the sense that I belong to someone." Or, "I'm thankful for God's grace, because I know that I make mistakes, and I need His help every day." Or, "I'm grateful for the Holy Spirit living inside me, because I really do want to live a holy life, and without Him*

*empowering me, I would never manage it." Paul urged us not to overlook these spiritual blessings because it is important to recognize the price that Jesus paid to provide them.*

**8.** *Some of the things we learn about God's nature from Ephesians 1:3–14 include: He chooses us as His children before we choose Him, He wants us to be in His family, He lavishes His grace on us, He is generous, He is self-sacrificing, and He is sovereign over everything that happens.*

**9.** *As believers, we have been made new in Christ! This is the root of our thankfulness. All the blessings God showers on us as His children come because of Jesus. We are not left on our own to deal with the world. Rather, we are joined to Christ and can have a moment-by-moment awareness of His Presence.*

**10.** *These concepts can become more real to us if we take the time to reflect on them. We can focus on just one word—chosen—and mull it over until it sinks deep into our hearts. Or we can talk about these ideas with another person until we get it. Journaling is another way to absorb these blessings into our hearts.*

**11.** *Answers will vary.*

**12.** *Answers will vary.*

**13.** *Responses will vary.*

## Session 6: Celebrating Your Life in Christ

**1.** *Later in the session, the group will look at the apostle Paul's answer to this question in 1 Corinthians 15:17–19. But for now, allow the group members to express their ideas and opinions on the importance of Jesus' resurrection.*

**2.** *Answers will vary. Some Christians regard every Sunday as Easter, so they are continually celebrating Jesus' resurrection and the new life they have been given.*

3. *Without gratitude, we tend to be suspicious toward Jesus, essentially asking, "What have You done for me lately?" while failing to clearly see the abundant answers to that question. We view Him through the distorted lens of our insatiable wants, which blocks our view of His beauty and goodness and trustworthiness. All these things get stripped away when we practice gratitude.*

4. *Some of us just seem to be born with a greater need to feel in charge of our worlds. Others among us felt powerless in our chaotic childhoods, so we crave control as adults. In either case, this ingrained habit needs to be overwritten with a new habit of yielding control to Jesus. We can build that habit by letting go of control in smaller areas and working our way up to bigger things. The Holy Spirit will help us in this process if we ask Him to do so.*

5. *If we are convinced that God is good, it changes our outlook on the struggles we are facing. As believers in Christ, we are secure in the knowledge that He will not let anything ultimately—eternally—harm us, even when we or our loved ones die. Those tragedies can still be woven into a tapestry of God's goodness, because death is not the final word in any believer's story. Beyond death there is resurrection. If we're convinced of that fact, then nothing in this life can threaten our well-being.*

6. *The Bible depicts Jesus as totally trustworthy: Christ said He would die and rise again— and He did die and rise again. The resurrection is evidence that God does what He says. He allowed some of His followers (such as Stephen) to suffer in order to demonstrate the strength of their faith to themselves and to outsiders; yet even when they died, He was with them (Acts 7:54–60). If we doubt the trustworthiness of Jesus, we can read the Gospels and the book of Acts to see how He persistently cared for people and fulfilled what He promised—and still does today. In addition, the entire history of the church tells of men and women who trusted in Jesus and experienced His Presence no matter what they went through.*

7. *Death is the penalty of sin. In dying, Christ paid the penalty for all who confess Him as Lord and Savior. In rising, He showed that He was greater than death. So if Christ was not raised, then death—the penalty for sin—has not been conquered and His death could not*

provide forgiveness of our sins. As Paul stated in Romans 4:25, "He was delivered over to death for our sins and was raised to life for our justification."

8. Paul put up with persistent pain during his traveling ministry to spread the gospel. He was arrested, beaten, robbed, shipwrecked, and endured many other sufferings (2 Corinthians 11:23–27). He endured all this because of his hope of eternal reward. The people to whom he preached likewise suffered persecution for their faith. They, too, endured injustice and looked forward to the ultimate justice they would receive in the next life. If that hope was empty, their lives were pitiable. All the sufferings of Christians are likewise endurable because of their confidence that God will heal everything in eternity.

9. "Fallen asleep" is a figure of speech referring to death. Those who have died with faith in Christ are not dead and gone but are with Christ now, waiting to be clothed again in resurrected bodies like His. Jesus' resurrection was the "firstfruits," or first portion, of a harvest to come: the resurrection of His followers. Jesus' resurrection is the evidence and guarantee that ours is coming. It guarantees that, for those of us who are believers, our sins really are forgiven and an abundant, wondrous future in heaven, reunited with loved ones who put their faith in Christ, really is our destiny. Contemplating what's in store for us should make us persistently joyful, regardless of our present circumstances.

10. In popular imagination, heaven is a place where disembodied people float around, play harps, sing endless (and not very interesting) songs, and don't do much else. However, with resurrected bodies, we look forward to doing all kinds of creative activity in a new earth full of the beauties of nature unravaged by sin. Our bodies will be strong, whole, and immortal. We will feast together and enjoy the wonder of God's Presence intimately.

11. Answers will vary.

12. Answers will vary.

13. Responses will vary.

# Experience a Deeper Relationship
## with Jesus Through the
### *Jesus Calling®* App

Get inspiring content for every day of the year! App users can read the *Jesus Calling® Magazine*, listen to the *Jesus Calling®* podcast, access other Sarah Young devotionals, browse readings by topic, take notes as you read, and more!

## Get started today for free.

# When it feels like no one listens,
# Jesus hears you.

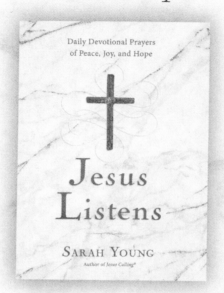

*Jesus Listens* is a 365-day daily prayer devotional from the best-selling author Sarah Young. It's the perfect companion piece to *Jesus Calling* with short, heartfelt prayers based on Scripture.

Look for these additional *Jesus Listens* titles.

**Jesus Listens Note-Taking**

**Jesus Listens 365 Prayers for Kids**

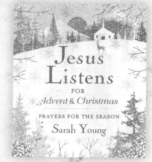

**Jesus Listens for Advent & Christmas**

# Explore the Jesus Calling®

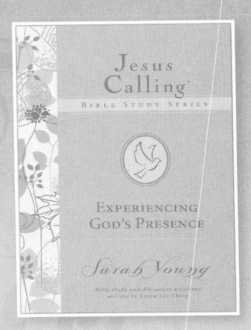

Jesus Calling®
BIBLE STUDY SERIES

EXPERIENCING
GOD'S PRESENCE

Sarah Young

Bible study and discussion questions
written by Karen Lee-Thorp

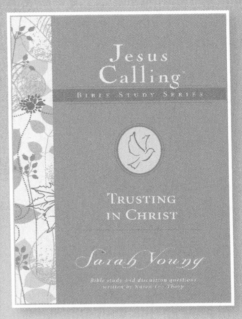

Jesus Calling®
BIBLE STUDY SERIES

TRUSTING
IN CHRIST

Sarah Young

Bible study and discussion questions
written by Karen Lee-Thorp

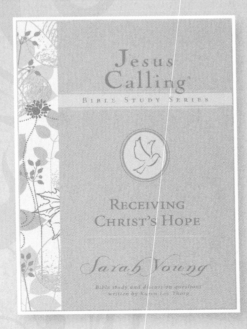

Jesus Calling®
BIBLE STUDY SERIES

RECEIVING
CHRIST'S HOPE

Sarah Young

Bible study and discussion questions
written by Karen Lee-Thorp

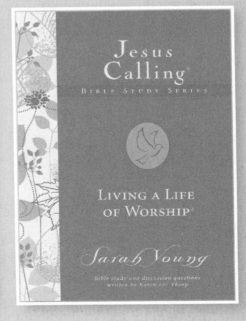

Jesus Calling®
BIBLE STUDY SERIES

LIVING A LIFE
OF WORSHIP®

Sarah Young

Bible study and discussion questions
written by Karen Lee-Thorp

# Bible Study Series

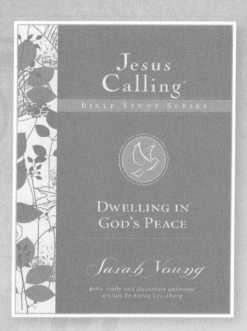

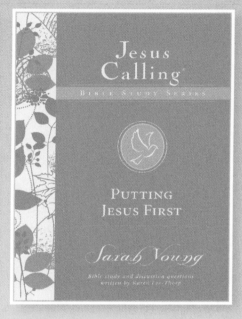

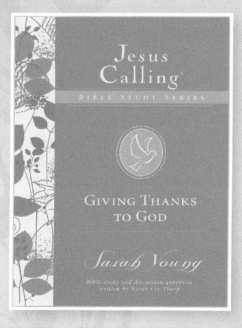

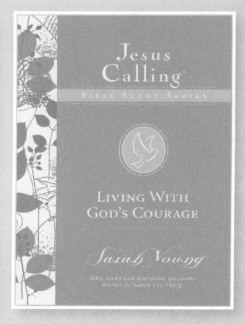

If you enjoyed this book, you may like
these additional devotionals by

*Sarah Young*

**Jesus Calling**
Enjoying Peace in His Presence
ISBN 9781591451884

**Jesus Today**
Experience Hope Through His Presence
ISBN 9781400320097

**Jesus Always**
Embracing Joy in His Presence
ISBN 9780718039509

JESUSCALLING.COM

# THE JESUS ALWAYS® BIBLE STUDY SERIES

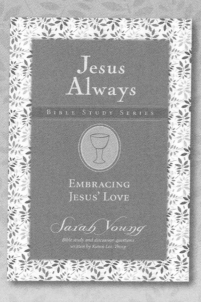

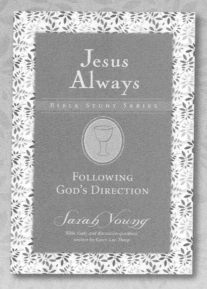

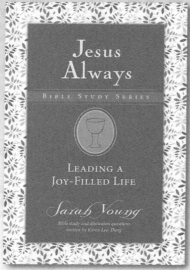

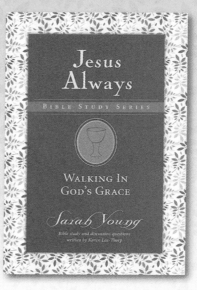